THE OFFICIAL
TOTTENHAM HOTSPUR

ANNUAL 2022

Written by Andy Greeves | Designed by Dan Brawn

A Grange Publication

© 2021. Published by Grange Communications Ltd., Edinburgh, under licence from Tottenham Hotspur Ltd. Printed in the EU.

Photographs © Getty Images

ISBN 978-1-913578-85-5

CONTENTS

WELCOME TO THE OFFICIAL TOTTENHAM HOTSPUR ANNUAL 2022

It's an exciting time to be a Spurs supporter, with Portuguese Head Coach Nuno Espírito Santo guiding our men's senior team while Rehanne Skinner leads our Barclays FA Women's Super League side.

This Annual profiles our star-studded squads and introduces our new summer signings. We find out how our players got on at the delayed UEFA Euro 2020 and 2020 Tokyo Olympic Games, while we reflect on our performances during the 2020/21 season.

We celebrate the club's 140th birthday on 5 September 2022 with an in-depth look at our rich history. Elsewhere, we go behind the scenes on a Tottenham Hotspur Stadium Tour while there are also quizzes, games, posters and plenty more besides.

**Enjoy your new Annual and
COME ON YOU SPURS!**

#COYS

Andy Greeves

140 YEARS
OF TOTTENHAM HOTSPUR

A look back at our long and illustrious history…

THE EARLY DAYS

On 5 September 2022 we celebrate the 140th anniversary of the foundation of Tottenham Hotspur Football Club. It was on that particular day back in 1882 that members of the Hotspur Cricket Club – who were pupils of St John's and Tottenham Grammar schools at the time - met under a gas lamp on Tottenham High Road to establish a football team to keep them busy during the winter months.

Originally named Hotspur Football Club, our first known match was a 2-0 defeat to a team called Radicals on 30 September 1882. Unfortunately there are no details of the team line-up or venue for that particular match. Our first known goal scorer, meanwhile, is Bobby Buckle, who netted in a 3-1 defeat to Grange Park on 20 October 1883.

Buckle is a significant figure in our history. One of the 11 schoolboys who formed the Club, Buckle was our first captain. He served as a member of the Club committee from 1884 and was appointed honorary secretary and treasurer in 1890. He was also elected to the first board of directors in 1898, having played an important role in our adoption of professional status three years earlier.

Buckle's home address – White Cottage on White Hart Lane – was used as our first postal address. Having started out playing our football on Tottenham Marshes, Buckle was involved with the club when we moved to Northumberland Park in 1888 and then assisted chairman Charles Roberts in securing the lease on a former nursery in 1899. John Over, groundsman at Edmonton Cricket Club, was hired to cultivate a football pitch at the ground which was to become known as White Hart Lane – the world famous home of the Spurs until 2017.

'61 SQUAD

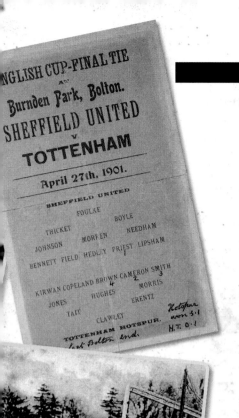

YEAR ENDS IN ONE

We enjoyed a number of major successes in our early history, most notably our FA Cup triumph in 1901. We were a Southern League team at the time, but we were able to overcome top-flight Football League opponents Preston North End, FA Cup holders Bury and West Bromwich Albion as well as fellow Southern League outfit Reading to reach the final. After drawing 2-2 with Sheffield United in the final, we beat the Blades 3-1 in the replay to become the first and only non-league side ever to win the FA Cup.

We were elected into the Football League Second Division in 1908/09 and we won promotion to the top-flight at the end of that campaign.

Having won the FA Cup for the first time in 1901, our canny knack for winning trophies when the year ends in a one continued in 1921 as we triumphed in the competition once again. We beat Bristol Rovers, Bradford City, Southend United, Aston Villa and Preston North End to reach the final, in which we beat Wolverhampton Wanderers 1-0 at Stamford Bridge.

There was more success with a year again ending in a one in 1951 as we became Football League champions for the first time. Arthur Rowe's side won 25 of their 42 First Division matches during the campaign, drawing 10 and losing just seven.

MR. TOTTENHAM →

THE DOUBLE

In 1960/61, under the management of the legendary Bill Nicholson, we became the first club of the 20th century to do the 'Double', as we won both the Football League title and the FA Cup. During the campaign, we became the first top-flight club ever to amass 50 points after just 29 matches under the old two points for a win system – equivalent to 74 points today.

We started the season with a 2-0 victory over Everton and followed that up with home and away successes against Blackpool and Bolton Wanderers as well

as triumphs over Blackburn Rovers, Manchester United, Arsenal, Leicester City, Aston Villa and Wolverhampton Wanderers. That run of results saw us become the first top-flight team ever to win 11 consecutive league matches at the start of a campaign. A draw at Manchester City, followed by wins against Nottingham Forest, Newcastle United, Cardiff City and Fulham also saw us become the first side since Preston North End's 'Invincibles' of 1888/89 to be unbeaten for 16 matches at the start of a top-flight season.

We ended the campaign having won 31, drawn four and lost seven matches. Our final points tally of 66 (97 points today) saw us equal Arsenal's previous record set in 1930/31, while we matched the Gunners' record of 33 points amassed from away games in 1930/31 that campaign. **> > >**

We also became the first top-flight side ever to win 31 league matches in a single season.

Our FA Cup campaign began with a 3-2 victory at home to Charlton Athletic in the third round, then was followed by a 5-1 triumph over Crewe Alexandra at White Hart Lane and a 2-0 away win at Aston Villa. After a 1-1 draw at Sunderland, we won 5-1 in the quarter final replay in N17. A 3-0 win over Burnley in our Villa Park semi-final secured our first-ever Wembley appearance, where we beat Leicester City 2-0 on 6 May 1961 – with strikes from Bobby Smith and Terry Dyson – as we won the FA Cup and completed the elusive 'Double'.

There was further success a year later as we beat Burnley in the 1962 FA Cup Final to retain the trophy. Jimmy Greaves, who had signed from AC Milan in December 1961 for a fee of £99,999, scored in the 3-1 success. Greaves went on to become our all-time top goal scorer with 266 goals in 379 competitive matches for us through until 1970.

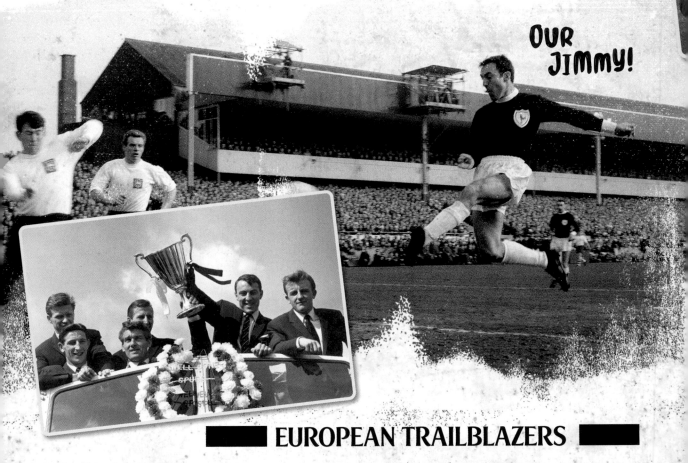

OUR JIMMY!

EUROPEAN TRAILBLAZERS

On 15 May 1963, we beat Atletico Madrid 5-1 in the European Cup Winners' Cup Final to become the first British club to win a major European trophy.

Braces from Jimmy Greaves and Terry Dyson, along with a further goal from John White, saw us to victory at Feyenoord's 'De Kuip' stadium in Rotterdam, with a crowd of 49,000 present for the showpiece final. Our road to European glory during the 1962/63 season began with an 8-4 aggregate victory over Rangers in the first round. Bill Nicholson's side then beat Slovan Bratislava of the former Czechoslovakia 6-2 on aggregate in the quarter-finals, while we overcame OFK Beograd of the former Yugoslavia with a 5-2 aggregate triumph in the semi-final.

Our success under Nicholson continued in 1967 as we beat Chelsea 2-0 in the first FA Cup Final to be played between two London clubs. Jimmy Robertson and Frank Saul scored in the Wembley showdown after we had beaten Millwall, Portsmouth, Bristol City, Birmingham City and Nottingham Forest to reach the final.

UEFA CUP 1971/72

Having first entered the Football League Cup in 1966/67, we were winners of the competition just five years later. Martin Chivers – one of the greatest forwards in our history with 174 goals in 367 appearances between 1968 and 1976 – netted twice in our 2-0 win over Aston Villa in the 1971 final. 'Big Chiv' also bagged a brace in the first leg of the inaugural UEFA Cup Final against Wolverhampton Wanderers in 1972. Having won 2-1 at Molineux, our 1-1 draw with Wolves at White Hart Lane in the second leg was enough to see us win the trophy 3-2 on aggregate.

Our third major final in as many years saw us beat Norwich City 1-0 in the 1973 League Cup Final at Wembley thanks to a strike from substitute Ralph Coates. But a few months after our 1974 UEFA Cup Final defeat to Feyenoord, Bill Nicholson departed as manager. Some difficult seasons followed, which included relegation to the old Second Division in 1977. Spurs bounced back though, and returned to the top flight just a year later, marking their promotion by signing two Argentinian World Cup winners – Ossie Ardiles and Ricky Villa.

The duo played a major role in us winning the FA Cup in 1981. Villa's winning goal in the 3-2 FA Cup Final replay victory over Manchester City – a mazy dribble past four City defenders and finish under goalkeeper Joe Corrigan – was subsequently voted 'Wembley Goal of the Century' in 2001. Keith Burkinshaw's side returned to Wembley 12 months later and won the FA Cup once again, beating Queens Park Rangers 1-0 in the final replay thanks to a penalty from one of the club's finest ever players, Glenn Hoddle.

Hoddle, along with goalkeeper Ray Clemence, was unable to play a part in our 1984 UEFA Cup Final against Anderlecht due to injury. In addition, Ardiles missed the first leg while skipper Steve Perryman was suspended for the second leg, which added to the uphill task the team faced against Belgian side Anderlecht. After a 1-1 draw in Brussels, stand-in captain Graham Roberts scored in a 1-1 draw in the second leg at White Hart Lane to force extra-time – and, eventually, penalties. Rookie goalkeeper Tony Parks saved two spot-kicks as we triumphed 4-3 in the shoot out to win the third major European trophy in our history.

BIG CHIV

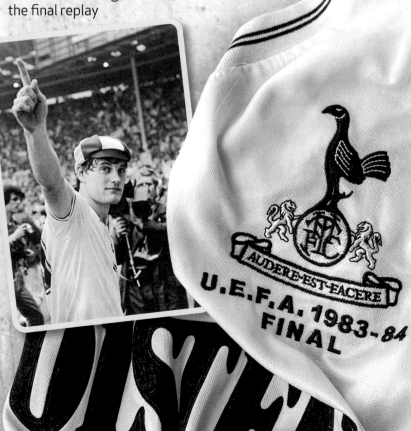

U.E.F.A. 1983-84 FINAL

The last decade of the 20th century began in predictable fashion, as we won yet another trophy when the year ended in a one. Our memorable run to the 1991 FA Cup Final included a 3-1 victory over rivals Arsenal in the semi-final at Wembley, which featured a wonderful free-kick from Paul Gascoigne and a brace from Gary Lineker. 'Gazza' got injured early in the final against Nottingham Forest around the same time we went 1-0 down to a Stuart Pearce free-kick. But Terry Venables' side rallied and we ran out 2-1 winners after extra-time thanks to a strike from Paul Stewart and an own-goal from Des Walker.

The following year, we were one of 22 founder members of the Premier League. To date, we are one of only six teams to have remained in the division for every single season since – alongside Arsenal, Chelsea, Everton, Liverpool and Manchester United. Our second trophy success of the 1990s occurred in 1998/99 as we beat Leicester City 1-0 in the League Cup Final – the same season in which our French winger David Ginola was named both the Professional Footballers Association and Football Writers Association Player of the Year.

LEAGUE CUP '08 →

We won the League Cup once again in 2008, as Jonathan Woodgate headed our extra-time winner against Chelsea at Wembley. Two years later, we sealed our first qualification to the UEFA Champions League by virtue of a fourth-place finish in the Premier League in 2009/10. Our run to the quarter-finals of the competition the following season saw Gareth Bale announce himself as a major star of the world game, not least because of his hat-trick against reigning European champions Inter Milan.

WEDNESDAY 3 APRIL 2019

Memories

UCL 2018/19

We were back in the UEFA Champions League in 2016/17; the same season we said goodbye to our home of 118 years. Under the management of Mauricio Pochettino, our team signed off in style – completing an entire season without suffering defeat in N17 and finishing second in the Premier League.

Pochettino's side temporarily played 'home' matches at Wembley as the construction of the 62,850-seat Tottenham Hotspur Stadium was completed. One of highlights of our stay at the national stadium was a 3-1 victory over the reigning European champions Real Madrid in the UEFA Champions League in November 2017.

A stunning fireworks display heralded the official opening of Tottenham Hotspur Stadium in April 2019, as we beat Crystal Palace 2-0 in our first Premier League match at our new home. Days later, we beat Manchester City 1-0 there in the UEFA Champions League first-leg quarter-final. By virtue of the away goals rule, a 4-3 defeat at the Etihad Stadium saw us through to a memorable semi-final meeting with Ajax. Trailing 1-0 from the first leg, we trailed 3-0 on aggregate by half-time of the second leg in Amsterdam. But a famous Lucas Moura hat-trick turned the tie on its head and ensured our place in an all-English final against Liverpool which, sadly, we lost 2-0 in Madrid.

We competed in the UEFA Champions League for a fourth consecutive season in 2019/20, while our most recent cup final appearance came in 2021 as we took part in the Carabao Cup Final against Manchester City (see pages 16-19 for more details).

PREMIER LEAGUE
SEASON REVIEW
— 2020/21 —

The 2020/21 campaign saw us secure a 12th consecutive season in European competition. We will compete in the newly-formed UEFA Europa Conference League in 2021/22 by virtue of our seventh-place finish in the Premier League. We won 18 and drew eight of our 38 league matches during the season, amassing 62 points. Harry Kane collected the division's Golden Boot and Playmaker awards having scored 24 goals and made 14 assists in the Premier League during the season

SEPTEMBER

As a result of the late finish of the 2019/20 Premier League season, the 2020/21 campaign didn't get underway until mid-September. We went down to a 1-0 home defeat to Everton on the opening weekend of the season but we bounced back the following week with a 5-2 triumph at Southampton. Heung-Min Son scored four times in our victory at St Mary's and Harry Kane was also on target.

We then looked set for back-to-back Premier League victories as we led from a Lucas Moura goal at the end of the 90 minutes in our clash against Newcastle United at Tottenham Hotspur Stadium. Seven minutes into stoppage time though, Callum Wilson levelled for the Magpies from the penalty spot.

Our most memorable result and performance of the season came at the start of October as we hammered 13-time Premier League champions Manchester United 6-1 at Old Trafford. We went behind after just two minutes to a Bruno Fernandes penalty but strikes from Tanguy Ndombele and Kane, plus a brace from Son gave us a 4-1 half-time lead. The Reds' Anthony Martial was also sent off during the first-half. Our control of the game continued after the break as Serge Aurier made it 5-1 and a Kane penalty 11 minutes from time rounded off our victory.

We were three goals up after just 16 minutes of our home match against West Ham United as Son and Kane (two goals) found the back of the net. However in a real 'game of two halves', a Fabian Balbuena header, an own goal from Davinson Sanchez and a long-range effort from Manuel Lanzini rescued a point for the Hammers late on.

Son was on target again as we secured a 1-0 win at Burnley the following week.

OCTOBER

NOVEMBER

Gareth Bale scored his first goal for us since his loan return to Spurs from Real Madrid in our 2-1 win over Brighton & Hove Albion at Tottenham Hotspur Stadium. A penalty from Kane gave us a half-time lead against the Seagulls, who equalised after the break through Tariq Lamptey. Bale came on as a 70th-minute substitute for Erik Lamela to head our winner with his first strike in our colours in seven years and 166 days.

Our fine run of form continued with a 1-0 success at West Bromwich Albion, which featured a late Kane goal. We then climbed to the top of the Premier League table on the back of a magnificent 2-0 home win over eventual season champions, Manchester City. Son netted after five minutes of the game while Giovani Lo Celso scored in the second half, just 35 seconds after coming on as a substitute for Ndombele.

DECEMBER

We maintained our place at the top of the Premier League table after a trio of London derbies. A goalless draw at Chelsea was followed by a 2-0 home triumph over Arsenal. Son and Kane scored in the first half of the match against the Gunners, with 2,000 spectators granted access for a league fixture at Tottenham Hotspur Stadium for the first time that season. A limited number of supporters – albeit home fans only – were also present as we drew 1-1 with Crystal Palace at Selhurst Park, Kane scoring his ninth Premier League goal of the campaign.

Son's league goal tally moved up to 11 as he got our equaliser at Liverpool. Alas, a late score from Roberto Firmino saw the Reds leapfrog us in the table, while a disappointing week was completed by a 2-0 home loss to Leicester City.

Our first match after Christmas saw us draw 1-1 at Wolverhampton Wanderers, with Ndombele on target at Molineux.

JANUARY

The new year began with a 3-0 triumph over Leeds United at Tottenham Hotspur Stadium. A penalty from Kane and further strikes from Son and Toby Alderweireld delivered a deserved three points for Jose Mourinho's team. We were frustrated in our home match with Fulham though, as a 74th-minute Ivan Cavaleiro goal secured a point for the visitors after we had led for much of the game through Kane's opener.

Following this, there was a return to winning ways at Sheffield United. Ndombele scored the pick of our goals with an audacious lob over Blades goalkeeper Aaron Ramsdale, while Aurier and Kane also netted in our 3-1 triumph at Bramall Lane.

Unfortunately late January saw Pierre-Emile Højbjerg's impressive 20-yard drive come in vain as we went down to a 3-1 home defeat to Liverpool, while a disappointing 1-0 away loss at Brighton & Hove Albion followed.

FEBRUARY

We bounced back from a third consecutive Premier League defeat at the hands of Chelsea with a 2-0 home success against West Bromwich Albion. Our dynamic duo, Kane and Son, were on target once again in the victory over the Baggies.

A 3-0 reverse at Manchester City and a 2-1 defeat at West Ham United followed, with Lucas getting our goal in the latter fixture. After back-to-back losses, the month ended on a high as we beat Burnley 4-0 at Tottenham Hotspur Stadium. Bale got a brace while Kane and Lucas both scored against the Clarets.

MARCH

Dele Alli's goal-bound effort deflected off Tosin Adarabioyo to give us a 1-0 win at Fulham while we made it three consecutive Premier League victories with a 4-1 triumph over Crystal Palace in N17. Bale and Kane got two goals apiece against the Eagles.

Lamela then scored a 'goal of the season' contender with a 'rabona'-style strike against Arsenal at the Emirates Stadium. Unfortunately, it wasn't enough to secure us a result as we went down to a 2-1 defeat to our north London rivals.

Brazilian striker Carlos Vinícius, who joined us for a season-long loan from Benfica in 2020/21, scored his first Premier League goal in our 2-0 win at Aston Villa, with Kane also netting.

APRIL

As was the case when the sides met at Tottenham Hotspur Stadium earlier in the season, a late Newcastle United equaliser denied us all three points when we visited St James' Park. A brace from Kane gave us a 2-1 lead after Joelinton's opener, but Joe Willock scored with four minutes of the 90 remaining to give the Magpies a share of the points.

We led our home clash with Manchester United at half-time through a Son goal, but the visitors rallied in the second period to run out 3-1 winners. In our next game, Kane's second Premier League brace of the month helped us to a 2-2 draw at Everton.

Danny Ings gave Southampton a half-time lead as they visited Tottenham Hotspur Stadium towards the end of the month. Former Saint Gareth Bale levelled in the second half and a last-minute penalty from Son gave us a 2-1 victory.

MAY

A busy May saw us play five Premier League fixtures in 22 days. The month got off to an excellent start as we beat Sheffield United 4-0 at Tottenham Hotspur Stadium. Bale scored a hat-trick in the game – his first league trio for us since his treble in a 4-0 win at Aston Villa in December 2012. Son was also on target in our comfortable win over the Blades.

Next, we visited Elland Road for a Premier League match for the first time since January 2004. Son scored for a third consecutive game but it was Leeds United who took the points with a 3-1 victory. Goals from Kane and Højbjerg then saw us return to winning ways as we triumphed 2-0 against Wolverhampton Wanderers.

A home clash with Aston Villa saw a welcome return of fans to Tottenham Hotspur Stadium for the first time since we hosted Arsenal back in December 2020. Some 10,000 supporters saw us take an early lead as Steven Bergwijn scored his first goal of the season. Alas, Villa ended up winning 2-1.

The curtain came down on our Premier League campaign at Leicester City's King Power Stadium. The Foxes twice led the game through Jamie Vardy penalties. A strike from Kane and an own goal from Kasper Schmeichel drew us level on each occasion before Bale came off the bench to give us all three points with a quick-fire brace against that season's FA Cup winners.

THE ROAD TO WEMBLEY

CARABAO CUP 2020/21 REVIEW

One of the highlights of the 2020/21 season was our run to the final of the Carabao Cup. Here's a look back at our journey to Wembley and the showpiece final against Manchester City.

Third Round
Leyton Orient W/O Spurs

Brisbane Road
22 September 2020

Due to multiple Leyton Orient players testing positive for COVID-19, our proposed third round tie at Brisbane Road on 22 September 2020 had to be postponed. In the days that followed, the English Football League issued a statement which read; "in line with Carabao Cup Rule 5.1, the Club (Leyton Orient) was unable to fulfil its obligations to complete the fixture by virtue of the Council's order and shall therefore forfeit the tie" and that "in accordance with Carabao Cup Rules, Tottenham Hotspur have been awarded with a bye to progress to round four of the Carabao Cup".

The fourth round draw handed us a home match against fellow Londoners, Chelsea.

Spurs 1-1 Chelsea
(Spurs win 5-4 on penalties)

Tottenham Hotspur Stadium
29 September 2020

Chelsea dominated proceedings in the first half of our fourth round clash in N17 and took the lead on 19 minutes through Timo Werner, who bagged his first goal for the Blues.

Jose Mourinho's men rallied in the second half though and debutant Sergio Reguilon forced a fine save from Chelsea goalkeeper Edouard Mendy shortly after the break. Reguilon then played a key role in our equaliser, which came seven minutes from time, as he crossed for Erik Lamela to slot home at the back post.

With the scores level at the end of 90 minutes, the match was settled with a penalty shootout. Eric Dier, Lamela, Pierre-Emile Højbjerg and Lucas Moura all scored their spot-kicks for Spurs while Tammy Abraham, César Azpilicueta, Jorginho and Emerson responded in kind for Chelsea. Harry Kane, who had come on as a 70th-minute substitute for Japhet Tanganga, showed typical composure to place our fifth penalty beyond the reach of Mendy. Mason Mount put his subsequent effort wide to send us through to the next round.

TEAMS

Spurs: Lloris, Tanganga (Kane 70), Alderweireld, Dier, Aurier, Sissoko, Gedson (Højbjerg 63), Ndombele, Reguilon, Lamela, Bergwijn (Lucas 76)

Chelsea: Mendy, Chilwell (Emerson 66), Tomori, Zouma, Azpilicueta, Hudson-Odoi, Jorginho, Kovačić (Kanté 70), Mount, Giroud (Abraham 76), Werner

Stoke City 1-3 Spurs

Gareth Bale scored his third goal of the 2020/21 season in a third different competition as he gave us the lead against Stoke City with a flicked header from a Harry Winks cross. The Welshman had already netted against Brighton & Hove Albion in the Premier League and LASK in the UEFA Europa League in a campaign that saw him score 16 goals in 34 appearances overall.

Potters goalkeeper Andy Lonergan made a series of good saves in the game – twice from Dele Alli and once from Kane – before the home side equalised in the second half through Jordan Thompson.

A 25-yard drive from Ben Davies restored our lead at 70 minutes, while Moussa Sissoko provided the assist for Kane to complete our 3-1 win 11 minutes later.

TEAMS

Stoke City: Lonergan, Collins, Souttar, Batth, Smith, Cousins, Thompson, Fox (Fletcher 34), Oakley-Boothe (Vokes 79), Brown (Powell 71), McClean

Spurs: Lloris, Doherty, Sanchez, Dier, Davies, Højbjerg, Winks, Bale (Son 45), Dele (Lamela 66), Lucas, Kane

Semi Final
Spurs 2-0 Brentford

Tottenham
Hotspur Stadium
5 January 2021

We welcomed Brentford to Tottenham Hotspur Stadium in January 2021 for the Bees' first major cup semi-final of their history.

The EFL Championship side had beaten four Premier League clubs en route to that season's last four, but they went behind on 12 minutes to Sissoko's header from a Sergio Reguilon cross. The west Londoners were denied an equaliser in the second half when Ivan Toney's headed 'goal' was ruled out for offside. On 70 minutes, Heung-Min Son made sure of our place in the final with a run and composed finish past David Raya, before Bees defender Josh Dasilva saw red for a foul on Højbjerg with six minutes left.

TEAMS

Spurs: Lloris, Aurier, Sanchez, Dier, Reguilon (Davies 71), Sissoko, Højbjerg (Tanganga 86), Lucas (Winks 71), Ndombele, Son, Kane

Brentford: Raya, Dalsgaard, Pinnock, Sørensen, Henry, Dasilva, Janelt (Marcondes 74), Jensen, Mbeumo (Forss 81), Toney, Canós (Fosu-Henry 74)

Manchester City 1-0 Spurs

Our eighth League Cup Final also happened to be a re-run of the 1981 FA Cup Final, as we took on Manchester City at Wembley in front of a restricted crowd of 7,773.

City had the better of the early chances prior to Toby Alderweireld's low shot just wide of Zack Steffan's goal on 20 minutes. At the other end, Hugo Lloris continued to make a series of fine saves as the first half progressed. Two minutes into the second period, Giovani Lo Celso had our best effort of the afternoon, as he sent a curling strike towards the bottom corner of the Citizens' goal which Steffan managed to keep out with his outstretched right hand.

Bale came on as a 67th-minute substitute as we continued to search for the opening goal, but it was City who got the all-important opener on 82 minutes as Aymeric Laporte headed past Lloris from a Kevin De Bruyne free-kick for the win. Pep Guardiola's side retained the Carabao Cup for a fourth consecutive season as a result.

TEAMS

Manchester City: Steffen, Walker, Dias, Laporte, Cancelo, De Bruyne (Silva 87), Fernandinho (Rodri 84), Gündoğan, Mahrez, Sterling, Foden

Spurs: Lloris, Aurier (Bergwijn 90), Alderweireld, Dier, Reguilon, Winks, Højbjerg (Dele 84), Lucas (Bale 67), Lo Celso (Sissoko 67), Son, Kane

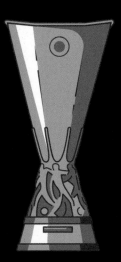

UEFA
EUROPA LEAGUE

OUR 11TH CONSECUTIVE SEASON IN EUROPEAN COMPETITION IN 2020/21 SAW US PROGRESS TO THE LAST 16 OF THE UEFA EUROPA LEAGUE

QUALIFYING ROUNDS

Second Qualifying Round
Lokomotiv Plovdiv 1-2 Spurs

Our UEFA Europa League campaign began in Bulgaria as we took on national cup winners, Lokomotiv Plovdiv. The hosts took a 71st-minute lead through Georgi Minchev but were reduced to nine men just seven minutes later as both Bircent Karagaren and Dinis Almeida were sent off. Harry Kane levelled from the penalty spot with ten minutes of the 90 remaining and Tanguy Ndombele scored our winner just five minutes later.

Third Qualifying Round
Shkëndija 1-3 Spurs

Erik Lamela gave us a fifth-minute lead at the Toše Proeski Arena in Skopje against North Macedonian side Shkëndija. The 'Red and Blacks' equalised in the second-half thanks to a strike from Egzon Bejtulai but goals from Heung-Min Son and Harry Winks saw us through to the Play-Off round.

Play-Off Round
Spurs 7-2 Maccabi Haifa

A dominant display, which included a Kane hat-trick, saw us progress to the Europa League group stage. Tjaronn Chery equalised for the Tottenham Hotspur Stadium visitors after Kane's second-minute opener. Lucas Moura put us back in front and a brace from Argentinian international Giovani Lo Celso saw us leading 4-1 at half-time. A Nikita Rukavytsya penalty reduced the arrears for Maccabi Haifa on 52 minutes but a spot-kick from Kane and a further strike made it 6-2 by 74 minutes. A Dele Alli penalty rounded off our 7-2 win in stoppage time.

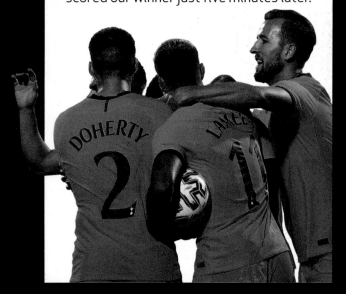

Matchday One
Spurs 3-0 LASK

Carlos Vinicius impressed on his Spurs debut as we saw off the challenge of Austrian side LASK with relative ease at Tottenham Hotspur Stadium. The striker, on loan from Benfica, set Lucas Moura up for our opener on 18 minutes while he also provided the assist for our third goal on the evening, scored by Heung-Min Son. In between, LASK defender Andrés Andrade inadvertently put Gareth Bale's low ball into the back of his own net as Vinicius was in a prime position to score.

Matchday Two
Royal Antwerp 1-0 Spurs

Israeli international Lior Refaelov gave Royal Antwerp maximum points with a first-half strike at the Bosuilstadion. It was our first away defeat in any competition since a 3-1 loss to Sheffield United in July 2020.

Matchday Three
Ludogorets 1-3 Spurs

Harry Kane scored his 200th goal in our colours as he scored our opener against Bulgarian outfit Ludogorets after 13 minutes. Lucas put us two up by the break while Lo Celso added a third in the second half as we moved top of the Group J table.

Matchday Four
Spurs 4-0 Ludogorets

Vinicius got his first Spurs goals since his loan move from Benfica on 16 and 34 minutes, as we completed back-to-back victories over Ludogorets. A long-range effort from Winks increased our lead in the second period while Lucas rounded off the 4-0 win on 73 minutes.

LASK 3-3 Spurs

We twice led but had to settle for just one point as we visited the Linzer Stadion in Linz, Austria. Peter Michorl opened the scoring for the home team just before the break but Gareth Bale levelled from the penalty spot in first half stoppage time. Son gave us the lead on 56 minutes but Johannes Eggestein levelled on 84 minutes. Dele's 86th-minute penalty looked like it would be good enough for victory until Mamoudou Karamoko equalised for LASK in the third minute of stoppage time.

Spurs 2-0 Royal Antwerp

There was a welcome sight at Tottenham Hotspur Stadium as a small number of our supporters were permitted into the stadium after months of 'behind closed doors' matches due to COVID-19 restrictions. Vinicius gave the fans something to cheer on 57 minutes with his third Europa League goal of the season. Lo Celso's strike on 71 minutes confirmed our progression to the knockout phase of the competition as Group J winners.

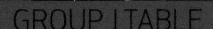

GROUP J TABLE

		P	W	D	L	GF	GA	GD	PTS
1	Spurs	6	4	1	1	15	5	+10	13
2	Royal Antwerp	6	4	0	2	8	5	+3	12
3	LASK	6	3	1	2	11	12	−1	10
4	Ludogorets	6	0	0	6	7	19	-12	0

Round of 32, first leg
Wolfsberger 1-4 Spurs

Originally scheduled to be played at Wörthersee Stadion in Klagenfurt, Austria, our round of 32, first-round tie against Wolfsberger was moved to Puskás Aréna in Budapest, Hungary due to COVID-19 restrictions. Bale set up our 13th-minute opener for Son and then scored our second goal in the Hungarian capital on 28 minutes. Lucas also netted in the first half while Vinicius was on target with two minutes of normal time remaining to seal our victory. Michael Liendl got Wolfsberger's consolation from the penalty spot.

Round of 16, first leg
Spurs 2-0 Dinamo Zagreb

Kane scored in both halves to give us the upper hand in our two-legged tie against Dinamo Zagreb. The England captain was on hand to tap in a rebound after Lamela's effort struck a post on 25 minutes. He scored his 26th club goal of the season on 70 minutes before limping off late on with a knock to his knee.

Round of 32, second leg
Spurs 4-0 Wolfsberger
(Spurs win 8-1 on aggregate)

Dele's incredible overhead kick put us on course to complete a comfortable 8-1 aggregate victory over Wolfsberger after just 11 minutes of the round of 32, second leg tie. Bale scored in between a second half brace from Vinicius as we ran out 4-0 winners on the night at Tottenham Hotspur Stadium.

Round of 16, second leg
Dinamo Zagreb 3-0 Spurs (AET)
(Dinamo Zagreb win 3-2 on aggregate)

A virtuoso performance from Mislav Oršić saw us exit the Europa League in disappointing fashion. The Croatian international, who was included in his country's squad for UEFA Euro 2020, gave his side some hope of overturning their first leg deficit with a curling, right-footed effort on 62 minutes. His second strike on 83 minutes took the game into extra-time and he completed his hat-trick in the added period of 30 minutes with a fine individual goal.

THE FA CUP

2020/21 REVIEW

Third Round
Marine 0-5 Spurs

The FA Cup third round draw took us to Marine of the Northern Premier League Division One West in January 2021. The non-leaguers, who play at the eighth level of English football's league pyramid, started brightly and rattled Joe Hart's woodwork with a 25-yard effort from Neil Kengni after 20 minutes. We took command of the tie thereafter with four goals in 13 first-half minutes. Brazilian forward Carlos Vinicius bagged a hat-trick while his compatriot Lucas Moura also netted. Sixteen-year-old substitute Alfie Devine came off the bench in the second half to score on his debut and complete our 5-0 victory.

Fourth Round
Wycombe Wanderers 1-4 Spurs

We were given an early scare by Championship side Wycombe Wanderers when their midfielder Fred Onyedinma slotted home from close range after 25 minutes of the Adams Park clash. After hitting the woodwork twice in the first half, we finally equalised in stoppage time at the end of the first 45 minutes as Gareth Bale hooked a Lucas Moura cross into the back of Ryan Allsop's net. Harry Winks' long-range effort gave us the lead with four minutes of the 90 remaining and a brace from Tanguy Ndombele completed a comfortable victory in the end.

Fifth Round
Everton 5-4 Spurs (AET)

We were involved in yet another high-scoring FA Cup contest that season but sadly it was Everton who came out in front after a nine-goal thriller at Goodison Park in February 2021. Davinson Sánchez gave us the lead after just three minutes but Everton responded with strikes from Dominic Calvert-Lewin, Richarlison and a Gylfi Sigurdsson penalty. Erik Lamela got a goal back in first half injury time before Sánchez equalised in the second period with his second goal of the night. Richarlison put the Toffees back in front, completing a brace of his own, before Harry Kane forced extra-time with a strike with seven minutes left on the watch. It was Brazilian international Bernard who got Everton's winner in the first period of extra-time.

2020/21
YOUTH TEAM ROUND-UP

Our development teams competed in a variety of competitions during the 2020/21 season...

PREMIER LEAGUE 2

Wayne Burnett's U23 side were in impressive form during the 2020/21 Premier League 2 season, finishing third in the division. The young Lilywhites won 11 of their 24 league fixtures, drawing five and losing eight matches.

Season highlights included a 4-3 away win over Liverpool in December 2020, featuring a brace from Jubril Okedina, and goals from Brooklyn Lyons-Foster and Jack Clarke. We beat the Reds 4-1 in the corresponding fixture, played at Tottenham Hotspur Stadium in April 2021, with a double strike from Elliot Thorpe and further efforts from Alfie Devine and Dilan Markanday.

UNDER-18 PREMIER LEAGUE

Matt Taylor's side were involved in a host of high-scoring matches during the 2020/21 Under-18 Premier League season, including home wins over Southampton (7-0) and Norwich City (5-2), a 5-1 victory at Crystal Palace and a 4-4 draw with Reading.

Having beaten Arsenal 2-0 at home earlier in the campaign, our U18s also chalked up another triumph over another of our London rivals, thrashing Chelsea 6-1 at their Cobham Training Ground in March 2021. Roshaun Mathurin scored a hat-trick against his former club in the game. We ended the season in sixth position in the table with 10 wins, seven draws and seven defeats.

FA YOUTH CUP

Dane Scarlett scored five goals as our Under-18s came back from a 2-0 deficit to beat Newport County 6-2 in an FA Youth Cup third round tie at Hotspur Way. Roshaun Mathurin was also on target in the game. Dane made his senior Premier League debut soon after that game, coming on as a substitute in our 2-0 victory over West Bromwich Albion at Tottenham Hotspur Stadium in February 2021. He also previously featured in our UEFA Europa League triumph over Ludogorets Razgrad in November 2020.

Three goals in extra-time saw us beat Wimbledon in a hard-fought fourth round encounter at Plough Lane in March 2021. Two strikes from Romaine Mundle, plus one from Jamie Donley, saw us to a 3-0 victory. We exited the competition in the next round, going down in a heavy 5-0 home defeat to West Brom.

TOTTENHAM HOTSPUR WOMEN

2020/21 REVIEW

Our second successive season in the Barclays FA Women's Super League (WSL) saw us finish eighth in the top division of women's league football. The campaign featured WSL victories over the likes of Aston Villa, Birmingham City and West Ham United, the loan arrival of FIFA Women's World Cup winner Alex Morgan and a run to the quarter finals of the Women's FA Cup.

SEPTEMBER

An own-goal from Grace Fisk helped us to a 1-1 draw against West Ham United at our regular home for the season, The Hive, in our opening WSL fixture of the campaign. In between that game and our 1-0 away defeat at Everton, we announced the signing of United States international Alex Morgan on loan from Orlando Pride until the end of the calendar year. Morgan was working her way back to fitness at the time, having given birth to her daughter Charlie earlier in 2020.

OCTOBER

A difficult month saw us lose three consecutive WSL fixtures – away to Manchester City and Arsenal, then at home to Manchester United. Goals from Ria Percival, Alanna Kennedy, Rosella Ayane and Angela Addison gave us something to cheer though as we beat London City Lionesses 4-0 at home in the FA Women's League Cup.

NOVEMBER

After a 2-0 defeat to Chelsea in the League Cup, we were able to secure back-to-back draws in the WSL. Ashleigh Neville got our goal as we drew 1-1 with Reading at The Hive – a game in which Morgan made her long-awaited debut as a substitute - while Dutch international Siri Worm and Neville were on target in our 2-2 tie at Bristol City.

A solid performance saw us twice come from behind to draw 2-2 at Arsenal in the League Cup. Percival and

Canadian defender Shelina Zadorsky scored in the game that ultimately saw us lose 5-4 on penalties.

November also saw Karen Hills and Juan Amoros depart as head coaches to be replaced by ex-England women's assistant manager Rehanne Skinner.

DECEMBER

Skinner got off to the perfect start with us, with back-to-back WSL victories. Morgan got her first Spurs goal from the penalty spot to wrap up our 3-1 victory over Brighton & Hove Albion at The Hive. Kerys Harrop and Addison netted earlier in that game. The American also scored a penalty in our 3-1 home win over Aston Villa – a match that featured a Caroline Siems own-goal and a strike from Ayane.

JANUARY

With Birmingham City unable to field a team for our WSL meeting early in the new year, we were awarded a victory in that particular fixture. Lucy Quinn then got the only goal of the game as we won 1-0 at West Ham United, before the month ended with a heavy 4-0 loss at Chelsea.

FEBRUARY

A 1-0 defeat at Aston Villa and a 3-2 home loss to Everton made February a month to forget for Skinner's side. Addison and Gemma Davison got our consolation goals against the Toffees.

MARCH

A 2-0 reverse at Brighton & Hove Albion was followed by two important WSL draws away to Reading and at home to Bristol City. A stalemate against the Royals came prior to a 1-1 tie with the Robins – a game in which Worm got our goal. The month ended with a 3-0 defeat to rivals Arsenal at Tottenham Hotspur Stadium.

APRIL

Owing to the effects of the COVID-19 pandemic, the Women's FA Cup fourth round was staged in April rather than January. We twice came from behind in a pulsating tie away to Reading, with Kennedy and Rachel Williams on target to force extra-time at the Madejski Stadium. In the added period of 30 minutes, Jessica Naz popped up with our winner.

We suffered two defeats in the WSL during the month – a 3-0 home reverse to Manchester City and a 4-1 away loss at Manchester United.

MAY

Our WSL season ended with a 2-0 home defeat to Chelsea followed by a 1-0 win at Birmingham City – a game in which Kit Graham scored our winner.

Progress in the Women's FA Cup continued with a 2-1 extra-time victory over Sheffield United at The Hive. Quinn and Graham were on target to set up a quarter final match away to Arsenal. The tie against the Gunners, scheduled for September 2021, was played after this Annual went to print.

2021/22 PLAYER PROFILES

Hugo Lloris

The 2021/22 season marks Hugo's tenth campaign in our colours, having joined us from Olympique Lyonnais back in 2012. Our club captain broke Darren Anderton's Premier League appearance record for us as he lined up in his 300th match in the division against Wolverhampton Wanderers in August 2021. Lloris also holds our Premier League clean sheet record, with 104 shutouts in the division prior to the start of the 2021/22 campaign. At international level, the goalkeeper has played over 100 times for France and captained them to FIFA World Cup glory in 2018.

Pierluigi Gollini

Pierluigi joined us on a season-long loan from Italian side Atalanta prior to the start of the 2021/22 campaign. Standing at 1.94m (6ft 4in) tall, the Bologna-born goalkeeper previously represented Hellas Verona and Aston Villa, and starred for Atalanta during their memorable UEFA Champions League campaign in 2019/20. He made his senior international debut for Italy in November 2019 as he came on as a substitute for Gianluigi Donnarumma in a 3-0 victory over Bosnia and Herzegovina.

Sergio Reguilón

September 2020 was a busy month for Sergio, as he joined us from Real Madrid, made his Spurs debut against Chelsea in the Carabao Cup and made his senior international debut for Spain. The Madrid-born left-back made his first Premier League appearance in our memorable 6-1 away win over Manchester United in October 2020 during a campaign in which he featured in 36 matches for us.

Cristian Romero

Cristian joined us on loan from Atalanta for the 2021/22 season on the back of having been named Serie A's best defender during the previous campaign. Born in Cordoba, Argentina, the centre-back started his career at Club Atlético Belgrano before joining Genoa in 2018 and moving on to Juventus a year later. He was part of Argentina's victorious squad at the 2021 Copa America and started in La Albiceleste's 1-0 win over Brazil in the final of the competition.

Joe Rodon

Following his move from Swansea City in the summer of 2020, Rodon featured in 14 matches for us during the 2020/21 season. After making his debut as a substitute against Burnley in October 2020, his first start came in a goalless draw at Chelsea the following month. He was selected in Wales' squad for the delayed UEFA Euro 2020 alongside teammate Ben Davies and former Spur, Gareth Bale.

Davinson Sánchez

Prior to the arrival of Tanguy Ndombele, Davinson was our club record signing, having joined from Ajax in August 2017. The Colombian international has since gone on to feature in over 150 matches for us in all competitions, including eight appearances during our memorable run to the UEFA Champions League final in 2018/19. At international level, he has played over 40 times for Colombia and was part of their squad which finished third at the 2021 Copa America.

Eric Dier

Dier was closing in on 300 Spurs appearances at the start of the 2021/22 season, having joined us from Sporting Lisbon back in August 2014. The versatile player, who is able to operate in defence or midfield, scored the winning goal for us on his Premier League debut against West Ham United later that month. The England internationalput pen-to-paper on a new four-year contract with us in July 2020.

Ben Davies

Born in Neath on 24 April 1993, Davies rose through the ranks at Swansea City to establish himself as a first-team regular. He made 85 senior appearances for the Swans between 2012 and 2014 before his move to us in the summer of 2014. The Welsh international has since gone on to play over 225 matches for us. He signed a new five-year contract in July 2019.

Matt Doherty

The Dublin-born defender previously played for our Head Coach Nuno Espírito Santo during his time at Wolves. He scored a total of 28 goals in 302 appearances for Wolves between 2011 and 2020, during which time he was also loaned to Hibernian and Bury. The right-sided player, who made his debut for us against Everton in September 2020, has represented the Republic of Ireland at U19, U21 and senior international level.

Emerson Royal

Brazilian international defender Emerson – full name, Emerson Aparecido Leite de Souza Junior - signed for us from Barcelona on transfer deadline day in August 2021. The São Paulo-born right-back made his senior breakthrough at Ponte Preta. He signed for Atlético Mineiro in April 2018 and the following January joined Real Betis in Spain, making 79 appearances and scoring five goals over the next two-and-a-half seasons. Following his participation at the 2021 Copa America with Brazil, Barcelona acquired his services and he made three La Liga appearances for them at the start of the current season.

Japhet Tanganga

Tanganga progressed through our youth ranks to make his first-team debut against Colchester United in the Carabao Cup in September 2019. The defender made 11 appearances during the 2019/20 season, with his Premier League baptism coming against Liverpool in January 2020. The England U21 international followed that up by making 13 appearances in 2020/21 and began the 2021/22 campaign in impressive fashion, collecting the Man of the Match award after our 1-0 triumph over Manchester City on the opening weekend of the season.

Oliver Skipp

Skipp returned to Spurs prior to the start of the 2021/22 campaign following a successful loan spell with Norwich City the previous season. The midfielder scored once in 47 appearances for the Canaries in 2020/21 and was named in the PFA Championship Team of the Year as a result of his performances. The England U21 international made his Spurs debut in our 3-1 Carabao Cup victory at West Ham United in October 2019 and put pen-to-paper on a new three-year contract with us in July 2020.

Ryan Sessegnon

Sessegnon returned to Spurs before the start of the 2021/22 season after a productive loan spell with Bundesliga side 1899 Hoffenheim, for whom he scored twice in 29 appearances in 2020/21. The left-sided player joined us from Fulham in the summer of 2019, having netted 25 times in 120 appearances for the Whites between 2016 and 2019. The Roehampton-born player made his debut for us in a 1-1 draw with Everton in November 2019.

Tanguy Ndombele

A new arrival prior to the start of the 2019/20 season, Ndombele scored on his competitive debut for us in a 3-1 victory over Aston Villa in August 2019. The midfielder, who signed for us from Olympique Lyonnais in July 2019, netted twice in 29 matches in his inaugural season with us and followed that up with six goals in 46 appearances in 2020/21. A product of EA Guingamp's youth academy, Tanguy made his senior international debut for France against Iceland in October 2018.

Harry Winks

Winks' stand out moment of the 2020/21 season was a long-range goal against Bulgarian side Ludogorets Razgrad in the UEFA Europa League – a shot he hit from some 54 yards out! The lifelong Spurs fan started training with us from the age of five prior to making his first-team debut in our 1-0 victory over FK Partizan in the UEFA Europa League in November 2014. He had made 173 appearances for us in all competitions by the end of the 2020/21 season with four goals to his name. He made his senior England debut against Lithuania in October 2017.

Dele Alli

A two-time winner of the PFA's Young Player of the Year award (2016 and 2017), Dele has firmly established himself as a real fans' favourite since his 2015 move from MK Dons. By his high standards, the 2020/21 season was something of a disappointment for him, although he still managed to score three times in 29 matches. He made his 250th club appearance towards the end of that campaign against Aston Villa in May 2021.

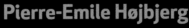

Pierre-Emile Højbjerg

Højbjerg enjoyed a memorable first season in our colours in 2020/21, appearing in all 38 of our Premier League matches. He scored twice in a total of 53 appearances for us that campaign, following a summer 2020 move from Southampton. The Dane impressed for his country at UEFA Euro 2020, featuring in all six of Denmark's matches as they reached the semi-final of the competition and was subsequently named in UEFA's 'Team of the Tournament'.

Lucas Moura

Lucas will forever be remembered for his hat-trick in our 3-2 UEFA Champions League semi-final, second leg victory over Ajax in May 2019, which took us to the final of the competition for the first time. The Brazilian international also holds the distinction of being the first hat-trick scorer at Tottenham Hotspur Stadium by virtue of his trio in a 4-0 win over Huddersfield Town in April 2019. The former São Paulo and Paris Saint-Germain player netted nine times in 50 matches for us during the 2020/21 season as he took his tally of club appearances over the 150 mark.

Steven Bergwijn

Dutch international Bergwijn made quite an impact at Spurs following his arrival from PSV Eindhoven in January 2020, as he scored on his debut in a 2-0 Premier League victory over Manchester City. He went on to score further goals against Wolverhampton Wanderers and Manchester United during the 2019/20 campaign, which saw him make 16 appearances for us in total. He then netted once in 35 appearances for us in 2020/21.

Jack Clarke

Able to operate as a winger or a forward, Clarke joined us from Leeds United in July 2019 and has since been loaned to a number of clubs, including Leeds, Queens Park Rangers and Stoke City. He made his senior debut for us in a UEFA Europa League match against LASK in October 2020 – one of three games he featured in for us during the 2020/21 season. Jack made his England U20 debut against Netherlands U20s in September 2019.

Giovani Lo Celso

Giovani was part of Argentina's victorious squad at the 2021 Copa America tournament, where he featured in six of La Albiceleste's seven matches, including the 1-0 win over Brazil in the final. Having impressed whilst on loan from Spanish club Real Betis in 2019/20, Giovani's Spurs contract was made permanent in January 2020. The creative midfielder previously played for Rosario Central and Paris Saint-Germain.

Bryan Gil

Bryan's signing from Sevilla was announced towards the end of July 2021, while the player was away representing Spain at the delayed 2020 Olympic Games. The winger featured in five matches at the tournament, helping his country win a silver medal in the process. Bryan departed Sevilla having scored twice in 21 appearances for the club between 2019 and 2021. Long-serving winger Erik Lamela departed N17 for Sevilla as part of his transfer.

Heung-Min Son

'Sonny' was a standout performer for us once again in 2020/21, as he netted 22 times in 51 appearances. His strike in our 3-0 win over Leeds United in the Premier League during the campaign saw him become just the 18th player in our history to have scored 100 or more goals for us. A two-time One Hotspur Player of the Season (2018/19 and 2019/20), the South Korean was just 20 appearances short of playing 300 matches for us prior to the start of the 2021/22 season. Memorable moments since the forward joined us from Bayer Leverkusen in 2015 includes his individual effort against Burnley in December 2019 that was subsequently named BBC Match of the Day's 'Goal of the Season' in 2019/20.

Harry Kane

Kane captained England during the delayed UEFA Euro 2020 tournament, with his extra-time, semi-final winner against Denmark sending the Three Lions to the final of a major competition for the first time in 55 years. At club level, the forward continues to close in on Jimmy Greaves' all-time goal scoring record for us. His 33 strikes in 49 appearances for us during the 2020/21 season took his goal tally for us to 221 – 45 short of 'Greavsie's' record of 266. He was the Premier League's top goal scorer in 2020/21 with 23 strikes and the top assist-maker with 14. He landed the Premier League's Golden Boot and Playmaker awards as a result.

UNLEASH
THE BRAVE

THE DARE
SKYWALK
EDGE

BOOK TICKETS NOW
EXPERIENCE.TOTTENHAMHOTSPUR.COM

NEW ARRIVALS
SUMMER 2021

The opening weekend of the Premier League campaign saw a trio of new players on our bench for our 1-0 victory over Manchester City at Tottenham Hotspur Stadium: Italian goalkeeper Pierluigi Gollini, Spanish winger Bryan Gil and Argentinian defender Cristian Romero, who had all joined us ahead of the start of the 2021/22 season.

Romero made his competitive Spurs debut in the game, introduced as a late replacement for Pierre-Emile Højbjerg. The centre-back, who will celebrate his 24th birthday on 27 April 2022, joined us on a season-long loan from Italians de Atalanta with an option existing to make his transfer permanent.

Born in Cordoba, Argentina, Romero started his career with local side Club Atlético Belgrano before moving to Italy to join Genoa in 2018. He moved to Juventus a year later, although he was instantly loaned back to Genoa and then spent much of the 2020/21 season on loan at Atalanta, where he was named the best defender in Serie A for that particular campaign. Atalanta secured his services on a permanent basis in 2021 before later agreeing to loan him to us for the 2021/22 season.

"I'm so happy to be here at this great club," said Romero, upon completing his transfer to Spurs. "From the moment I got the call I was sure it was the best option for me to keep improving and growing."

"I'M SO HAPPY TO BE HERE AT THIS GREAT CLUB"

Romero made his senior debut for Argentina in a 2022 FIFA World Cup qualifier against Chile on 3 June 2021. Later that month, he was included in Lionel Scaloni's 28-man squad for the 2021 Copa America, where he made three appearances. He started in

the final of the competition as Argentina beat hosts Brazil 1-0 at the Maracanã Stadium in Rio de Janeiro on 10 July 2021.

Like Romero, Gollini also arrived with us on a season-loan from Atalanta. The Bologna-born stopper was involved in the youth set-ups at Fiorentina and Manchester United prior to making his senior debut for Hellas Verona. He made 20 appearances for Aston Villa between 2016 and 2018 before going on to star for Atalanta in their memorable first season in the UEFA Champions League in 2019/20.

"This is an amazing feeling," commented Gollini on his arrival in N17. "I'm very happy for this opportunity. It's a massive club, a very good chance for me, a big chance. I'm really blessed and proud to be here. I'm so happy just to be part of this club and to join this team of great players."

Spanish international Gil joined us from Sevilla as part of a part-exchange deal that took winger Erik Lamela in the opposite direction. Having become part of Sevilla's youth set-up back in 2012, Gil rose through the ranks to eventually make his senior debut against Atletico Madrid in La Liga in January 2019. His goal against Rayo Vallecano in April 2019 saw him become the first player born in the 21st century to net in Spain's top-flight.

Gil made his senior Spain debut against Greece in March 2021 and represented his country at the delayed 2020 Summer Olympics (see page 46 for more details).

"I'M COMING TO SPURS TO WIN POINTS AND GIVE EVERYTHING"

"I'm very proud to join Spurs," said Gil, having completed his transfer. "To represent the badge of a world-class club like Tottenham and be able to play in the Premier League feels great. I'm coming to Spurs to win points and give everything in every minute. As a player, on top of hard work and sacrifice, I want to contribute dribbling, goals and assists."

Gil, Gollini and Romero all made their full debuts for us as they started in our UEFA Conference League play-off round, first leg tie away to Paços de Ferreira in August 2021.

UNREPEATABLE

AWAY KIT COLLECTION

SHOP SPURS

HOME OF OFFICIAL SPURS MERCHANDISE
TOTTENHAMHOTSPUR.COM/SHOP

WORDSEARCH

Can you find the surnames of EIGHT stars of our Women's team?
They can be any direction, including backwards…

M	P	L	T	D	K	O	R	P	E	L	A
T	P	B	C	R	L	T	N	M	Y	X	N
D	E	R	W	N	D	E	K	K	P	W	N
C	R	H	C	C	E	R	S	M	R	S	O
C	C	M	W	R	V	R	P	N	P	R	R
C	I	Z	G	V	O	X	B	E	A	D	A
Z	V	D	J	D	R	Q	N	K	M	Z	M
X	A	Y	A	X	T	C	M	K	L	X	E
P	L	Z	T	T	E	N	F	L	W	L	L
Z	L	R	V	R	B	F	M	Z	Q	G	C
K	Z	J	H	T	Q	N	Q	K	T	N	N
Y	F	Z	M	S	M	A	I	L	L	I	W

CLEMARON **NAZ** **WILLIAMS**

GREEN **PERCIVAL** **ZADORSKY**

KORPELA **SPENCER**

ANSWERS ON PAGES 61

PLAYER AWARDS

2020/21 SEASON

Harry Kane, Erik Lamela and Heung-Min Son were all rewarded for their efforts during the campaign.

On the back of a wonderful 2020/21 season, in which he scored 33 goals in 49 appearances for us in all competitions, Harry Kane was named our One Hotspur Members' Player of the Season, Junior Members' Player of the Season and our Official Supporters' Clubs' Player of the Season.

"It's great, I'm extremely thankful to everyone who voted," commented Kane on his trio of awards. *"It's been a good year from a personal point of view. It's nice to be scoring the goals and adding some assists there as well so it's a proud moment for me; it's nice to get these awards and of course it's a big thanks to the whole team."*

Kane also collected the Premier League's Golden Boot and Playmaker of the Season awards at the end of the 2020/21 campaign, having managed both the most goals (23 in 35 appearances) and the most assists (14) of any player in the division.

Erik Lamela won our Goal of the Season award for his incredible Rabona against Arsenal at the Emirates Stadium in March 2021. Having come on as a substitute for the injured Heung-Min Son, the Argentine international gave us the lead around the half-hour mark, wrapping his left foot around the back of his right to hook the ball through the legs of the Gunners' Thomas Partey and past goalkeeper Bernd Leno into the bottom corner. The strike brought back memories of another Rabona he scored for us in our 5-1 home win over Asteras Tripolis in the UEFA Europa League in October 2014.

"I'm happy to win this trophy and I want to say thank you to all the fans who voted for me – it's something special," said Erik, whose effort was also named the Premier League's EA SPORTS Goal of the Month for March 2021. *"Of course, it has a different feeling to do it in the derby – these games are completely different to other ones and it's a very, very special goal. Honestly, I just decided in that moment to shoot like that. It was one second. Of course, I dream a lot about goals like that, especially in a derby, but it was in one second that I decided to shoot like that."*

Heung-Min Son was named Player of the Season for 2020/21 by sponsors AIA. The South Korean international enjoyed his most productive Premier League campaign yet in terms of goals. His 17 top-flight strikes in 2020/21 put him fourth on the division's top scorers' list that campaign behind Kane (23), Liverpool's Mohamed Salah (22) and Bruno Fernandes (18) of Manchester United. In all, Sonny scored 22 goals in 51 appearances for us during the season.

PRE-SEASON ROUND-UP
SUMMER 2021

Following the appointment of Nuno Espírito Santo as our new Head Coach, summer preparations for the 2021/22 season began with a 1-1 draw with Leyton Orient at The Breyer Group Stadium. Dane Scarlett scored our opening goal of the match after 38 minutes, before substitute Ruel Sotiriou levelled for the O's with 18 minutes remaining. The result meant the two teams shared the JE3 Foundation Trophy, which was introduced in 2020 in memory of our legendary former defender and ex-Orient boss Justin Edinburgh.

A few days later, three first-half goals from Heung-Min Son, Lucas Moura and Dele Alli set us on the way to a comfortable 3-0 win over Colchester United at the JobServe Community Stadium. At the other end, goalkeeper Alfie Whiteman made a couple of superb saves on his first senior start for us.

It was fitting that Dele was made captain for the night the following week, as we headed to his former club, MK Dons, for the third match of pre-season. The England international set up Son for our opener on 35 minutes, before getting on the scoresheet himself on 57 minutes. Lucas

also netted in our 3-1 win before youngster John Freeman got a late consolation for the home side in front of a crowd of 15,795.

Our pre-season preparations concluded with two matches in The Mind Series. Alongside London rivals Arsenal and Chelsea, we united with charity Mind to set up a friendly tournament to raise vital funds and promote mental health awareness.

Chelsea triumphed 2-1 at Arsenal in the tournament opener prior to our 2-2 draw at Stamford Bridge. We trailed 2-0 in SW6, as Hakim Ziyech scored twice for the Blues. But Lucas' third goal of pre-season coupled with a strike from Steven Bergwijn gave us a credible draw against the European champions in a match which marked goalkeeper Pierluigi Gollini's Spurs debut.

Arsenal visited Tottenham Hotspur Stadium for the final fixture of The Mind Series. After hitting the Gunners' woodwork three times, we finally made the breakthrough on 79 minutes as Son powered in a left-footed shot, having been setup by Japhet Tanganga. The 1-0 victory over our north London rivals completed an unbeaten pre-season.

So-hyun Cho

SPURS WOMEN NEW ARRIVALS
SUMMER 2021

Having bid a fond farewell to Rianna Dean, Alanna Kennedy, Gemma Davison, Anna Filbey, Hannah Godfrey, Lucía León, Aurora Mikalsen, Chloe Peplow, Lucy Quinn, Siri Worm and Elisha Sulola at the end of the 2020/21 season, the summer of 2021 proved a particularly busy time for our Women's Head Coach Rehanne Skinner. She oversaw the arrival of a host of new players, including a number of youth and senior internationals.

*Information correct as of 17th August 2021.

South Korean skipper **So-hyun Cho**, who has won over 125 caps for her country, made her move from West Ham United a permanent one in July 2021. Cho impressed in her eight appearances for us in all competitions in the second half of the 2020/21 campaign. The midfielder's arrival means our club is now home to the captain of both South Korea's men's (Heung-Min Son) and women's teams.

French midfielder **Maéva Clemaron** and Finnish goalkeeper **Tinja-Riikka Korpela** joined us from Everton. Clemaron made 19 FA Women's Super League (FA WSL) appearances for the Toffees between 2019 and 2021 while Korpela featured in 16 league matches during the same period. Both players

Asmita Ale

Tinja-Riikka Korpela

Maéva Clemaron

have been capped by their countries, with Korpela closing in on her 100th appearance for Finland at the time of writing.

A former Spurs youth player, **Molly Bartrip** returned to the club in July 2021 after a seven-year spell with Reading. The defender, who has been capped by England at various levels between U17 and U23, made 56 league appearances for the Royals having also previously trained with Charlton Athletic and Arsenal as a youngster.

July 2021 also saw us announce the signing of England U21 international **Gracie Pearce** from Crystal Palace. The defender put pen-to-paper on a two-year contract with us - with an option to extend for a further year - before being loaned back to Palace for the 2021/22 season.

London-born forward **Chioma Ubogagu**, who has played for some of the biggest clubs in the women's game including Orlando Pride, Brisbane Roar, Houston Dash and Real Madrid, signed a two-year contract with us. Capped by the United States between U18 and U23 level, Ubogagu switched her international allegiance to England in 2018 and has since won three caps*.

Chinese international **Tang Jiali** will spend the 2021/22 season on loan with us from Shanghai Shengli. First capped by her country at senior level back in 2014, midfielder Tang is a former Jiangsu Suning player. The daughter of a former Gurkha soldier, **Asmita Ale** is the first player of Nepalese origin to sign for a FA WSL club. The defender, who is an

England U19 international, arrived on a two-year contract from Aston Villa.

Having represented Australia at the delayed 2020 Olympic Games, **Kyah Simon** signed for us from Dutch side PSV Eindhoven. Simon has a century of Australian caps to her name and has represented the likes of Central Coast Mariners, Sydney FC, Boston Breakers, Western Sydney Wanderers, Melbourne City and Houston Dash during her career.

England U19 international goalkeeper **Eleanor Heeps** joined us after five years in the Liverpool academy where she progressed from U14 to the First Team level. She signed a contract until 2024 and joined FA Women's Championship side Blackburn Rovers on loan for the 2021/22 season.

Chioma Ubogagu

45

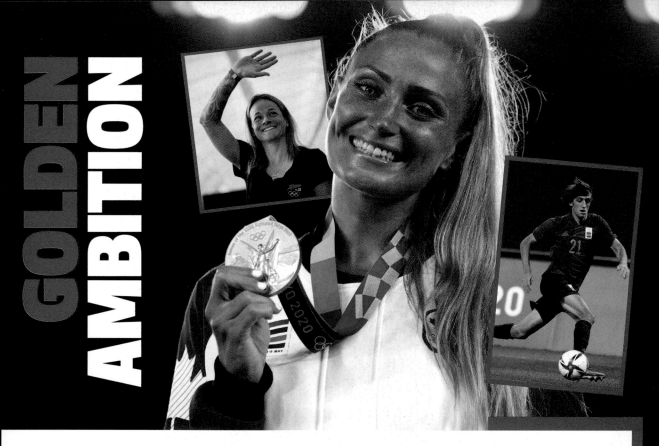

GOLDEN AMBITION

Three Spurs players took part in the football competition at the delayed 2020 Olympic Games which took place in the summer of 2021.

Originally scheduled to take place in 2020, the Tokyo Olympic Games were held in the summer of 2021, having been put on hold for a year due the COVID-19 pandemic.

Our Ontario-born defender Shelina Zadorsky was part of the first Canadian team to win gold in a football event at the Olympics since the men's side came out on top at the 1904 Games in St. Louis, United States. The women's team had previously taken bronze at the 2012 and 2016 Games.

Zadorsky started in two of Canada's three group games, as they drew 1-1 with Japan and beat Chile in Sapporo. She was an unused substitute for the 1-1 draw with Team GB in Kashima which saw Canada confirm a second-place finish in Group E and progress to

the knockout phase of the competition.

Shelina watched on as her team won on penalties in the quarter finals, beating Brazil 4-3 after a goalless match after extra time in Rifu. She was also an unused substitute for the 1-0 semi-final victory over the United States in Kashima. The Gold Medal Match pitted Canada up against Sweden in Yokohama. Zadorsky came on as an extra-time substitute for Desiree Scott shortly before the match went to a penalty shootout. Successful spot-kicks from Jessie Fleming, Deanne Rose and Julia Grosso saw Canada win 3-2 on penalties to claim gold, after the game had finished 1-1 after extra time.

Our summer signing Bryan Gil also reached the Gold Medal Match in the men's tournament. The winger appeared as a substitute in all three of Spain's Group C matches as they beat

Australia 1-0 in Sapporo and drew with both Egypt (0-0) and Argentina (1-1) to secure top spot in the group and progression to the quarter finals.

Gil again came off the bench during Spain's 5-2 last eight, extra-time victory over Ivory Coast in Rifu. Although he was an unused substitute in their 1-0 triumph over Japan in the semi-final in Saitama, he did come on as a second-half replacement for Marco Asensio in the 2-1 extra-time defeat to Brazil in Yokohama on 7 August 2021 as Spain took the silver medal.

Elsewhere at the Games, Ria Percival started all three Group G matches for New Zealand, as they went down to three consecutive defeats to Australia (1-2), the United States (1-6) and Sweden (0-2). Ex-Spur Alex Morgan also scored for the United States in New Zealand's heavy loss in Saitama.

ONE HOTSPUR
OFFICIAL MEMBERSHIP

JOIN AT
TOTTENHAMHOTSPUR.COM/MEMBERSHIP

BECOME ONE

- **PRIORITY MATCH TICKET ACCESS**

- **ONE HOTSPUR MOMENTS**

- **WELCOME GIFT**

EURO STARS

A total of eight Spurs players represented their countries at the delayed UEFA Euro 2020.

As a result of the COVID-19 pandemic, UEFA Euro 2020 was put on hold for a year and staged in the summer of 2021. The pulsating tournament - which featured 142 goals in 51 matches - was very much worth the wait…

The competition got underway in Rome where Italy beat Turkey 3-0 on 11 June. The following day, a trio of Spurs players – Ben Davies, Gareth Bale and Joe Rodon – started for Wales against Switzerland, which finished in a 1-1 draw. Bale and Rodon were ever-presents for the Dragons at Euro 2020. Rob Page's side finished second in Group A before suffering a 4-0 defeat at the hands of Denmark in the round of 16.

Our midfielder Pierre-Emile Højbjerg played a key role for the Danes, who eventually reached the semi-final of the competition. He appeared in all six of their matches, including their opening Group B match against Finland. It was during that game that our former midfielder Christian Eriksen suffered a cardiac arrest. We shared in world football's collective despair at the time and its subsequent relief to learn of his recovery. We continue to wish Christian and his family well.

Højbjerg – who was subsequently named in the UEFA Euro 2020 Team of the Tournament, along with five Italians, three Englishmen (including former Spur, Kyle Walker), Pedri of Spain and Romelu Lukaku from Belgium - came up against teammate Toby Alderweireld and ex-Spurs man Jan Vertonghen in Denmark's second Group B fixture. The game ended in a 2-1 win for Belgium. Alderweireld played in four of the Red Devils' five matches at Euro 2020, which saw them progress to the quarter-finals.

World champions France were many people's pre-tournament favourites to win the Henri Delaunay trophy. Skippered by our captain Hugo Lloris, Les Bleus made an instant impression by beating Germany 1-0 in their opening Group F match and topping their group after three games with subsequent draws against Hungary and Portugal. Didier Deschamps' side suffered a shock exit to Switzerland on penalties, though, after a memorable 3-3 draw after extra-time in a round of 16 clash in Budapest. Moussa Sissoko made two substitute appearances for France during the tournament.

England played their three Group D matches on home soil, with Wembley Stadium staging the Three Lions' clashes with Croatia, Scotland and the Czech Republic. Gareth Southgate's men got off to the perfect start with a 1-0 win over 2018 FIFA World Cup runners-up, Croatia. Harry Kane captained England – as he did in the next six matches as the Three Lions embarked on an epic run to the final.

A goalless draw with Scotland and a 1-0 win over the Czech Republic saw England top Group D. Kane's first tournament goal came in a memorable 2-0 win over Germany at Wembley in the round of 16, while he bagged a brace in the Three Lions' comfortable 4-0 win in the quarter-final against Ukraine in Rome.

England returned to Wembley for their semi-final encounter with Denmark. Mikkel Damsgaard put the Danes in front on the half-hour mark but a Simon Kjær own-goal nine minutes later eventually sent the match to extra-time. In the added period of 30 minutes, Raheem Sterling was adjudged to have been tripped by Joakim Mæhle in the 18-yard-box and referee Danny Makkelie awarded England a penalty as a result. Kasper Schmeichel saved Kane's original spot-kick but the Three Lions skipper responded quickly to fire in the rebound and send his team to their first-ever European Championships final.

Kane led England out at Wembley for their first major tournament final in 55 years against Italy on 11 June 2021. Less than two minutes in, our former player Kieran Trippier crossed for Luke Shaw to put the Three Lions one-up. Leonardo Bonucci levelled in the second half and the match eventually ended up going to extra-time and then penalties. Kane converted his spot-kick but it was the Azzurri who triumphed 3-2 on penalties to win their second European Championships.

FILL IN THE
BLANKS

Fill in the various gaps in information on these two pages from league tables and matches involving Spurs as well as our all-time top goal scorers list.

ANSWERS ON PAGES 60

LEAGUE TABLES

We finished seventh in the Premier League in 2020/21. Can you complete our goal difference and points total from that season's Premier League table?

Remember, three points are awarded for a win and one point for a draw!

		P	W	D	L	GF	GA	GD	PTS
7	SPURS	38	18	8	12	68	45	+ ☐	☐
8	Arsenal	38	18	7	13	55	39	+18	61
9	Leeds United	38	18	5	15	62	54	+8	59
10	Everton	38	17	8	13	47	48	-1	59

Fill in our missing opponents from the UEFA Europa Group B table in 2020/21. We have included the national flag of each club to give you a clue!

		P	W	D	L	GF	GA	GD	PTS
1	SPURS	6	4	1	1	15	5	+10	13
2	☐	6	4	0	2	8	5	+3	12
3	☐	6	3	1	2	11	12	-1	10
4	☐	6	0	0	6	7	19	-12	0

TOP GOAL SCORERS LIST

Fill in the names on our all-time, top goal scorers list
(Information correct prior to the start of the 2021/22 season)

	Player	Spurs Career	Club Apps.	Club Goals
1	J_____ G_____	1961-1970	379	266
2	H_____ K_____	2011-to date	336	221
3	B_____ S_____	1955-1964	317	208
4	M_____ C_____	1968-1976	367	174
5	C_____ J_____	1958-1968	378	159
6	J_____ D_____	2004-08 & 2009-14	363	143

ROAD TO WEMBLEY

Fill in the full-time scores from our Carabao Cup matches in 2020/21…

Fourth Round

Spurs ☐
Chelsea ☐
Spurs win on penalties ☐ - ☐

Quarter-final

Stoke City ☐
Spurs ☐

Semi-final

Spurs ☐
Brentford ☐

Final

Man City ☐
Spurs ☐

GOAL SCORERS

Fill in the missing goal scorers' name from selected Spurs Premier League victories in 2020/21…

Southampton 2
Ings 32', 90' (pen)

Spurs 5
_____ 45+2', 47', 64', 73',
Kane 82'

Spurs 2
Son 13',
_____ 45+1'

Arsenal 0

Manchester United 1
Fernandes 2' (pen)

Spurs 6
Ndombele 4', Son 7', 37',
Kane 30', 79' (pen)',
_____ 51'

Spurs 3
Kane 29' (pen), Son 43',
_____ 50'

Leeds United 0

Spurs 2
Son 5',
_____ 65'

Manchester City 0

Leicester City 2
Vardy 18' (pen), 52' (pen)

Spurs 4
Kane 41', Schmeichel (OG) 76',
_____ 87' 90+6'

CROSSWORD

Fill in the surnames of our UEFA Euro 2020 and 2020 Summer Olympics representatives from the following clues…

ACROSS

2. Australian, who also made her loan move from Orlando Pride permanent in 2021 - Alanna _____(7)

5. Canadian defender who made her loan move from Orlando Pride permanent in 2021 Shelina _____(8)

6. Welshman who spent the 2020/21 campaign with us on a season-long loan from Real Madrid - Gareth ____(4)

8. Defender who was included in the same squad as ex-Spur Jan Vertonghen at UEFA Euro 2020 - Toby _____(12)

10. Swansea-born defender who signed for us in 2020 - Joe _____(5)

11. Defender who signed for us from Swansea City in 2014 - Ben _____(6)

DOWN

1. Essex-born player who has played over 150 matches for New Zealand - Ria _____(8)

3. Captained England against Italy in the UEFA Euro 2020 Final - Harry ____(4)

4. Danish midfielder who played in all six of his country's matches at UEFA Euro 2020 - Pierre-Emile _____(8)

7. Frenchman who joined us from Newcastle United in 2016 - Moussa _____(7)

9. Captain of France - Hugo _____(6)

ANSWERS ON PAGES 61

NEW
HOME KIT

TOTTENHAM HOTSPUR
2021/22

SUPER SPURS
QUIZ

ANSWERS ON PAGES 61

1. **What year was the Club founded?**

2. **What nationality are So-hyun Cho & Heung-Min Son?**

3. **How many Spurs players were included in their national squads for UEFA Euro 2020?**

4. **Which Spurs player was included in UEFA Euro 2020 Team of the Tournament?**

5. **Who were our opponents in the 1963 European Cup Winners' Cup Final?**

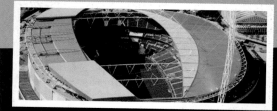

6. **Which stadium provided our temporary home while construction of Tottenham Hotspur Stadium was being completed?**

7. **Who scored a hat-trick in our famous 3-2 win at Ajax in the UEFA Champions League semi-final, second leg in 2019?**

8. **Which London clubs did we face in 'The Mind Series' in August 2021?**

9. **Which former Wolves manager was appointed as our new Head Coach in the summer of 2021?**

10. **Who were our opponents in the 2021 Carabao Cup Final?**

11. **Who were the two Argentinian World Cup winners we signed back in 1978?**

12. **Striker Carlos Vinicius joined us on loan during the 2020/21 season from which Portuguese club?**

13. **Which Dutch international scored on his Premier League debut for us against Man City in January 2020?**

14. **Which United States international scored her first Spurs goal against Brighton & Hove Albion in the FA WSL during a loan spell with us in 2020?**

15. Where did we play the majority of our FA WSL home matches in 2020/21?

16. Who took on the role as Head Coach of our Women's team in 2020?

17. What is the striking technique used by Erik Lamela to score his 'Goal of the (2020/21) Season' for us against Arsenal in March 2021 called?

18. Harry Kane collected the Golden Boot and which other award at the end of the 2020/21 season?

19. Which non-league side did we face in the FA Cup third round in January 2021?

20. Which country was Tanguy Ndombele born in?

21. Which adrenaline-packed attraction at Tottenham Hotspur Stadium allows you to step out onto a glass walkway 46.8m above the pitch?

22. Harry Kane and which other player scored braces in our 4-1 Premier win over Crystal Palace in March 2021?

23. What year did Tottenham Hotspur Stadium host its first Premier League match?

24. Underneath the football pitch at Tottenham Hotspur Stadium, there is a playing surface for which other sport?

25. Which historic, Grade II listed building is part of the Tottenham Experience?

26. What was the name of the cricket club Bobby Buckle and the other schoolboy founders of Spurs played for?

27. What is the name of our former French winger who won both the PFA & FWA Player of the Year awards in 1999?

28. Which competition did we qualify for in four consecutive seasons (2016 - 2020) reaching the final in 2019?

29. Ourselves, Arsenal, Chelsea, Liverpool, Manchester United and which other club have remained in the Premier League for every season since it was founded in 1992?

30. Who scored our match-winning goal in the 2008 Football League Cup Final?

BEHIND THE SCENES

Editor Andy Greeves and his five-year-old son Henry report on their experience of the Tottenham Hotspur Stadium Tour...

GETTING STARTED

The meeting point for visitors to the Tottenham Hotspur Stadium Tour is the Tottenham Experience at the southern end of the stadium - home to the largest retail space of any football club in Europe. It has a 100-seat auditorium, and it is here Henry and his dad Andy meet their tour host and watch an inspirational (or should that be in-spur-ational!) video prior to heading inside the stadium.

The first stop on the tour is the West Atrium – the main entrance to the stadium on a matchday. Here we find an array of treasures relating to the Club's history, including the FA Cup won in 1901, a collection of medals awarded to our players and a match ball from the 1961 FA Cup Final – an occasion which saw us beat Leicester City to become the first club of the 20th century to complete the league and cup 'double'. Also on display is a football, pennant and replica trophy from the 2008 Football League Cup Final success.

Additionally, the West Atrium has a time capsule (not to be opened until 2068) underneath the floor and covered by a glass panel. There is also a spectacular 69 metre-long, LED screen - the world's widest digital display in a reception area no less! Plus, you can check out the Club's historic clock, which was formerly attached to the 'Red House' building on Tottenham High Road before being restored to its former glory and taking up residence in the West Atrium.

DID YOU KNOW?

The Tottenham Hotspur Stadium is home to the largest retail space of any football club in Europe.

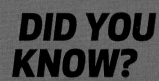
MOVING ON UP!

We head up two escalators to arrive at the middle tier of seating to take in a similar view experienced by Chairman Daniel Levy on matchday. After a first opportunity for us to take some photographs inside the stadium bowl, it's back down to the ground floor to check out the player facilities below.

One of the most interesting areas is the Home Warm-Up Room, which is located next to the Home Dressing Room and contains a range of equipment such as treadmills, weights and static bikes. Our audio headset, voiced by lifelong Spurs fan and Gavin and Stacey actor Mathew Horne informs us the players often commence their warm-ups here on a matchday. Henry reads aloud one of the motivational messages on the wall - 'Believe In Your Team Mates'!

The Home Dressing Room is one of the highlights of the tour, as you get the opportunity to sit in the same place your heroes do on matchday. There are 23 seating positions arranged in a horseshoe shape, which all face the centre of the room where the manager can address his players.

The pennants presented to us by our opponents ahead of big European matches can be found in the Away Dressing Room. There are various designs from our memorable UEFA Champions League run in 2018/19, which includes the one from our semi-final opposition, Ajax, as well as the Liverpool and UEFA-issue pennants from the 2019 Final in Madrid.

TUNNEL VISION

The Stadium Tour gives visitors the opportunity to undertake the famous walk from the Home Dressing Room, into the Players' Tunnel and out onto the pitch. Henry and I take a moment to stand in the tunnel area and we notice a dark mirrored wall to our right-hand side as we face towards the pitch. Behind that wall on a matchday is where members of the Tunnel Club can see the players gathering their final thoughts before they head out onto the pitch. While the 110 members can witness this, the players (and tour visitors!) cannot see back into the Tunnel Club!

DID YOU KNOW?

On a matchday, an inspirational video is shown on the stadium screens accompanied by the sound of John Williams' Duel of the Fates from the soundtrack for the original motion picture, Star Wars Episode I: The Phantom Menace.

As Henry heads out onto the pitch perimeter, he spots the golden cockerels either side of the doorway and the large letters spelling out 'COME ON YOU SPURS' in the Club's signature font. As you emerge from the tunnel and head up a slight incline, the view in front of you is truly breathtaking! We pause for a moment to imagine what the atmosphere must be like on matchday with a full capacity crowd. To our right, the South Stand is a majestic sight with its top row of seating some 34 metres above ground level. The single-tier stand holds an incredible 17,500 spectators – making it the biggest single-tier stand in the United Kingdom – with some 223 steps from the bottom of the South Stand to the top.

DID YOU KNOW?

The single-tier stand holds an incredible 17,500 spectators – making it the biggest single-tier stand in the United Kingdom.

TAKE A SEAT

While you're pitch side, you can take the opportunity to sit in the Home Dugout. There are 14 sports car-style 'bucket' seats, including the one occupied by Head Coach Nuno Espírito Santo on matchday. These seats are heated to keep everyone warm during chilly winter matches. Henry looks very serious as he pretends to instruct his Spurs team out on the pitch in front of him!

There are 31 padded, fold-down seats next to the Home Dugout, which are used by non-player squad members, medical staff, security personnel and observers from TV companies on matchdays. The Away Dugout is a similar layout to the Home one with comparable levels of comfort.

Heading back into the Players' Tunnel and along the main corridor, we arrive at one of the NFL Locker Rooms in the north-west corner of the ground (the other can be found in the East Stand). With 46 players in each NFL squad, plus coaching and backroom staff, cheerleaders and broadcasters, both Locker Rooms are HUGE and have been allocated around 500 square metres of space.

After visiting the 'Away' NFL Locker Room, we step inside the 120-seat, tiered Press Auditorium. Post-match press conferences take place here, allowing members of the written press and broadcasters to put questions to the home and away managers (with two separate conferences).

The Tottenham Hotspur Stadium Tour concludes with a visit to 'The M', which is used as the press lounge on matchdays and serves as a café at other times. Henry and I tucked into a stone-baked pizza at the end of an action-packed visit!

For more information and to book your tour, visit

www.tottenhamhotspur.com/ the-stadium/visitor-attractions/stadium-tours/

Please Note: The route taken on the Tottenham Hotspur Stadium Tour can vary and certain areas on the tour route may be out of bounds on occasions. Andy and Henry's tour took place in July 2021 when COVID-19 restrictions were in operation and their tour was self-guided as a result. Food and drink offered at The M is subject to the menu and availability.

ANSWERS

LEAGUE TABLES

W	D	L	GF	GA	GD	PTS
18	8	12	68	45	+23	62
18	7	13	55	39	+18	61
18	5	15	62	54	+8	59

		P	W	D
1	**SPURS**	6	4	1
2	Royal Antwerp	6	4	0
3	Lask	6	3	1
4	Ludogorets	6	0	0

TOP GOAL SCORERS LIST

	Player
1	Jimmy Greaves
2	Harry Kane
3	Bobby Smith
4	Martin Chivers
5	Cliff Jones
6	Jermain Defoe

ROAD TO WEMBLEY

Fourth Round

Spurs — 1
Chelsea — 1
Spurs win on penalties 5 - 4

Quarter-final

Stoke City — 1
Spurs — 3

Semi-final

Spurs — 2
Brentford — 0

Final

Man City — 1
Spurs — 0

GOAL SCORERS

Southampton 2
Spurs 5
Son (45+2', 47', 64', 73')

Spurs 2
Manchester City 0
Lo Celso (65')

Spurs 3
Leeds United 0
Alderweireld (50')

Manchester Utd 1
Spurs 6
Aurier (51')

Spurs 2
Arsenal 0
Kane (45+1')

Leicester City 2
Spurs 4
Bale (87', 90+6')

WORDSEARCH

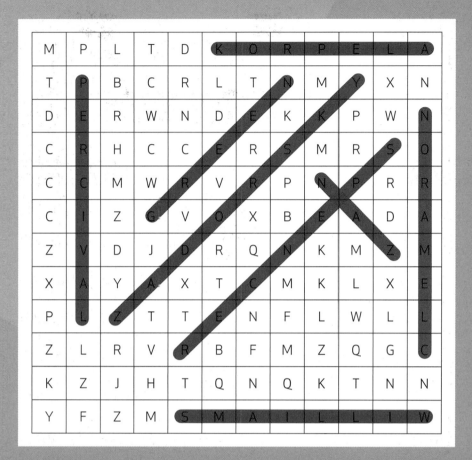

M	P	L	T	D	K	O	R	P	E	L	A
T	P	B	C	R	L	T	N	M	Y	X	N
D	E	R	W	N	D	E	K	K	P	W	N
C	R	H	C	C	E	R	S	M	R	S	O
C	C	M	W	R	V	R	P	N	P	R	R
C	I	Z	G	V	O	X	B	E	A	D	A
Z	V	D	J	D	R	Q	N	K	M	Z	M
X	A	Y	A	X	T	C	M	K	L	X	E
P	L	Z	T	T	E	N	F	L	W	L	L
Z	L	R	V	R	B	F	M	Z	Q	G	C
K	Z	J	H	T	Q	N	Q	K	T	N	N
Y	F	Z	M	S	M	A	I	L	L	I	W

CROSSWORD

ACROSS

2. Kennedy
5. Zadorsky
6. Bale
8. Alderweireld
10. Rodon
11. Davies

DOWN

1. Percival
3. Kane
4. Højbjerg
7. Sissoko
9. Lloris

SUPER SPURS QUIZ

1. 1882
2. South Korean
3. Eight
4. Pierre-Emile Højbjerg
5. Atletico Madrid
6. Wembley Stadium
7. Lucas Moura
8. Arsenal and Chelsea
9. Nuno Espírito Santo
10. Manchester City
11. Ossie Ardiles & Ricky Villa
12. Benfica
13. Steven Bergwijn
14. Alex Morgan
15. The Hive
16. Rehanne Skinner
17. Rabona
18. Playmaker of the Season
19. Marine
20. France
21. The Dare Skywalk
22. Gareth Bale
23. 2019
24. NFL/American Football
25. Warmington House
26. Hotspur Cricket Club
27. David Ginola
28. UEFA Champions League
29. Everton
30. Jonathan Woodgate